BADGER'S CRICKET COMPENDIUM

Badger's Cricket Compendium

A Humorous Treasury of Phrase & Foible

Niall Edworthy

Illustrations by Mudd Bexley

Publisher: Badger Books

ISBN: 978-1-7384522-0-0

Book design by Principal Publishing

nialledworthy.com

Biff —To hit the ball very hard.
See Also Slap, Smash, Cream, Crack, Wallop, Bash, Whack, Beast, Blast, Drub, Flay, Club, Hammer, Thrash, Cart, Smite, Batter, Leather, Crash, Spank, Bludgeon, Gazunder, Larrup, Smoke, Mallet

CONTENTS

Foreword .... *viii*

Abbreviations .... *x*

Aerial » Audi *1*

Back of a Length » Buzzers *3*

Cafeteria Bowling » Cut Him in Half *11*

Dab » Dustbowl *18*

Economy Rate » Eyeball *25*

Fag Paper » Furniture *29*

Gardening » Gun's Out of the Holster *35*

Half-tracker » Hutch *40*

Inroads » Knows Where His Off Stump Is *44*

Lappa » Lusty Blow *47*

Maiden » Mow *51*

Nelson » Nut *56*

Off for Light » Out to Graze *61*

Paddle » Quickie *64*

Radar » Rough *70*

Schoolboy » Swinging Like a Rusty Gate *73*

Tail » Two-eyed Stance *82*

Umbrella Field » Upstairs, Go *89*

Venom » Vultures *91*

Wahoo, Bit of a » Wrong 'Un *94*

X-Factor » Zone, in the *99*

Acknowledgements *103*

About the Author *105*

Foreword

THIS BOOK IS FOR the cricket enthusiast – the 'Badger' – not the neophyte. (**Neophyte.** *Noun. Formal.* New convert; newly initiated. Greek: 'newly planted'). It is not a textbook glossary of terms for the merely cricket-curious. Nor for the dandruffed pedant.

You will not find entries for the unusual but timeworn terms describing fielding positions, batsman's shots, bowling actions or any other common words that fill cricket's rich lexicon. If you don't know what is meant by Gully, Third Man, Short Leg, Right-arm Over, Box, Seamer, Square, Reverse Sweep … then this little glossary of terms will read like Serbo-Croat secret code.

The badger does not want to go down that rabbit hole and feed on such standard grub. He did all that when he was a cub. I hope what I have served here offers a feeding frenzy on more exotic fare.

The recent boom in television coverage and associated technology has led to a commensurate expansion in cricket terminology. Former players in the commentary box and the pundits' studio, post-match interviews with players, and live reporting on media websites have brought scores of neologisms into cricket vernacular. (**Neologism.** *Noun. Formal.* A new word or expression or a new meaning for an existing word. Greek: 'new word'). The compendium also includes the more eccentric or amusing terms that have been in circulation for many years.

It is not a serious book. Badgers will be familiar with most of the words and phrases, but I hope they will be entertained by the definitions given and the surprising etymology of some terms.

NE, Chichester 2024

Abbreviations

Arch. – Archaic

Aus. – Australian

Derog. – Derogatory

Dipl. – Diplomatic

Euph. – Euphemism

Hum. – Humorous

Mil. – Military

A

Aerial, Go — To take the risk of hitting a ball skywards, usually in the hope of clearing the boundary

Agricultural —*Derog. Hum.* Describing an awful hoick by a lower-order batsman, usually with a forgiving chuckle. Can be used to sum up a batsman's entire approach to the art of batting. Stems from the notion that all farmers, accustomed to crude and heavy work, deploy a bat as though it were a pitchfork or a flail

Air, Give it Some — What a spinner does when he gives the ball some **Flight**, bowling it a bit slower to force a mishit. A ball with 'some air' is an attacking one, inviting the batsman to gamble and have an expansive swing

Air Shot — Ugly waft at the ball, triggering a flurry of fanciful practice shots after the event, the batsman showing the crowd the classical version he normally plays

Amidships — *Euph.* Genital area, when a batsman is struck on the protective box. See also **Crown Jewels, Dress Circle, Knackers, Nether Region, Privates**

Approach Shot — *Derog.* A borrowing from golf describing a nothing-shot chipped into the outfield, usually between fielders

Arm Ball/With the Arm — Finger spinner's variation ball that doesn't spin but goes straight on. Stock delivery of the village 'spinner' who gets the ball to turn only when it hits a bump

Asterisk — Way of saying that a batsman is undefeated at the end of an innings or a day's play. e.g. *'That's another asterisk for Boycott to boost his series average.'* The idiom has its origins in media scorecards where the traditional symbol for a footnote informs the reader that the batsman is Not Out

Audi — *Hum.* Four consecutive ducks, or scores of zero suffered by a batsman, referring to the overlapping circles of the Audi marque

B

Back of a Length — Of a ball that pitches halfway down the wicket and rises between waist and shoulder height, i.e. short of a good length but not a bouncer and hard to score off

Badger — Extreme cricket enthusiast. A player who makes up for the absence of playing skills with an endearing exuberance for the game. Symptoms of 'Badgerism' manifest in a love of statistics, arcane knowledge and the irritating habit of correcting others and, in extreme cases, the collecting of autographs and the compilation of cricket dictionaries

Bag — Wickets taken by a bowler in an innings. Originated from the days when well-heeled amateur cricketers finished the cricket season, picked up their shotguns and set about bagging grouse and pheasant

Ball-Doctoring/Tampering — Illegally modifying the condition of the ball to alter its aerodynamic properties and aid the bowlers. Usually carried out with thumbnails, dirt, boot spikes and sun cream, but also bottle tops and sandpaper. See **Australians**

Ball on a String — To describe the mastery of line and length achieved by a spin bowler. Rarely uttered without an awe-struck sigh

Balloon — Ball that takes a looping trajectory as the result of an involuntary or poorly executed shot

Ball Talking, Get the — When a seam or swing bowler is moving the ball about and getting the batsman to play and miss and look like a clown

Banter – *Euph.* Word casting a light veil over the bitter exchange of insults taking place between the batsman and assorted fielders. See also **Niggle, Exchange of Pleasantries and Verbals**

Barnes Wallace — Ankle-height ball bouncing multiple times before reaching the batsman or the wicketkeeper accompanied by giggles, guffaws, and gasps. Rarely seen outside village greens. Refers to the inventor of the bouncing bomb used in the famous RAF raid on a German dam in 1944. See also **Dambuster**

Bat down to the Groundsman's Cat — Absurdist boast about a team's batting depth. Origin: probably Yorkshire

Bazball — Brand of fearless, high-risk cricket adopted under England coach Brendon 'Baz' McCullum and captain Ben Stokes, adopting an ODI mentality in a 5-day Test match. An ugly term for thrilling and nerve-wracking cricket

Beach Cricket — 1) Played on holiday to please an eight-year-old and involving the father in a marathon of ball-fetching and chasing of dogs 2) Commentator's disparaging description of a team batting in happy-go-lucky fashion. See also **Office Cricket**

Beauty — Superb delivery, usually unplayable

B&B pitch — Comfortable wicket for batting. All you have to do is turn up, check in and the runs are laid on. See also **Featherbed**

Bed of Snakes/Vipers — Opposite of a B&B pitch. A nightmare for batters, a paradise for bowlers, the ball darting, biting and spitting

Beehive —TV graphic showing varying height of balls bowled to a batsman. 'Beehive' because the balls depicted bear a dim resemblance to a swarm of bees

Beer Match — 1) Game tacked on at the end of a one-sided village or club game. 2) Commentator's contempt: *'You'd think this was a beer match!'*

Beer Snake — Northern pastime in which a fat, drunk man collects plastic pint glasses, generally during a dull passage of play. Mock tension mounts in the crowd and there is much hilarity when a final pint causes the wobbling snake to collapse

Belter — Very good wicket raising hopes of a) A well-balanced contest between bat and ball b) A fill-your-boots job for the batsmen

Bending the Back — Extraordinary effort put in by a pace bowler because a) It's a flat wicket offering nothing b) The team need to dig deep c) He's angry d) He doesn't like the batsman

Biff—To hit the ball very hard. **See Also** Slap, Smash, Cream, Crack, Wallop, Bash, Whack, Beast, Blast, Drub, Flay, Club, Hammer, Thrash, Cart, Smite, Batter, Leather, Crash, Spank, Bludgeon, Gazunder, Larrup, Smoke, Mallet

Big Lad — *Euph.* Fat bloke. Every village team has at least one. Often the unofficial team mascot. A Falstaffian figure in the outfield, he is often found at slip. Usually an 'agricultural' bat who gives it some **Biff**

Bite — Prodigious turn a spinner extracts from the wicket

Bits & Pieces Cricketer — *Derog.* Player who is not particularly good at anything. The sum of his parts, the 'bitzer' is useful in the shorter formats of the game. He will score 30, take a wicket or two, field tidily and occasionally produce a moment of magic out of nowhere to the astonishment of his teammates

Blow, Take a — Captain's polite instruction to a bowler who has been carted all around the ground and has probably bowled his last ball of the day. e.g. *'Thanks, Pat. Good effort. Why don't you take a blow down at fine leg?'*

Blob — Slang for a Duck

Blockhole — The small area around a batsman's boots into which a fast bowler fires a **Yorker** or **Toesmasher**

Boot Hill — Fielding at short-leg, the most dangerous position usually handed to the most junior player. Refers to the crude cemeteries of the Wild West where outlaws and cowboys died with their boots on in violent circumstances

Bosie — *Aus.* Googly, a spinner's ball that turns in the opposite direction to which the batsman is expecting. Named for its inventor, Englishman Bernard Bosanquet, a 1905 Wisden Cricketer of the Year

Bowlers' Graveyard — Lifeless wicket with absolutely no encouragement for bowlers, giving rise to an interminably dull, high-scoring game. Batsmen love them, bowlers despair. Often found on the sub-continent. See also **B&B wicket, Featherbed**

Box of Tricks — Skillset unique to a bowler, usually in reference to a spinner tying a hapless batsman in knots on a wicket favourable to his guile

Brisk — Wry understatement for a very fast bowler or a particularly quick ball that has almost decapitated a batsman

Bronze — Third-ball **Duck**

Brute — Extremely fast ball that has jumped from nowhere and startled the batsman into ungainly evasive action

Buffet Bowling — Bowling so awful the batsman can help himself and pile up the runs as he might his plate at the sideboard of a freebie lunch. See also **Cafeteria Bowling**

Bumper — *Arch.* Old-fashioned word for a bouncer, the short-pitched fast ball directed at the batsman's head

Bunny — Batsman at a perennial loss against a particular bowler. Like a bunny rabbit in the middle of the road, he is dazzled and frozen by the bowler's brilliance or psychological stranglehold, his life at the wicket soon to be cut short

Bunsen — Rhyming slang: Bunsen Burner – turner. A wicket offering extravagant spin

Bunt — Term borrowed from baseball. An unorthodox, usually ugly little shot sometimes yielding a single

Buzzers — Overthrows. Origin uncertain, but possibly from 'moll-buzzer', US street slang for a pickpocket

C

Cafeteria Bowling — See **Buffet Bowling**

Calypso Collapso — Crazy, self-destructive batting by a team leading to their rapid demise for a low score. Origin: Tabloid headlines inspired by England batting against the great West Indies' teams of the 1980s

Camel — Graceless and unathletic fielder, often an ageing fast bowler, dispatched to a distant backwater of the outfield in which he is least likely to make a fool of himself

Carpet — Another word for the pitch, but with two very different meanings: a) A playing surface that is lush green and therefore exciting for bowlers or b) One so flat and uniform a batsman will hope to fill his boots with runs

Cart Horse — See **Camel**

Castled — Colourful term, possibly borrowed from Chess, meaning to be clean-bowled by a fast bowler. Often used when the middle stump has been removed from the soil leaving only the off and leg ones standing, like turrets

Chalk End — Borrowed from Snooker & Pool to describe a shot stubbed with the toe end of the bat. See also **Cue End**

Channel — Usually prefixed by 'right' or 'wrong' to describe the line found by a bowler

Check Upstairs — When the on-field umpire refers a decision via his headset to the 'Third Umpire', or 'TV Umpire,' who uses technology devices to determine the outcome

Cheeky — Usually in reference to an unlikely single run taken when a fielder is idling or day-dreaming

Cherry — A new ball, lovely, red and shiny

Chin Music — *Euph.* Terrifying fast ball or bowling that shoots close to a batsman's head, sometimes making a whistling sound as it goes

Chinaman — Ball bowled by a left-arm spinner that moves into a right-hand batsman. Considered offensive and racist in some quarters, the term is sliding into disuse

Chinese Cut — Or French Cut, Surrey Cut or Harrow Drive. An involuntary shot that takes the inside edge of the bat and shoots perilously close to the stumps, often eluding the outstretched glove of a cartwheeling

wicketkeeper and flying away to the boundary. A source of deep and perennial annoyance to the bowler, prompting a nervous grin from the batsman

(Around the) Corner — Shot tickled, paddled, swept or glanced into the leg side, usually quite fine and into an area where there is no fielder to intercept it

Chirping — Like sparrows in a hedgerow. A mild version of **Sledging** perfected by wicketkeepers and close fielders, aimed at distracting the batsman and poking fun at his cricketing abilities, his current form, or his wife

Chunter — Grumbling and mumbling in the middle of the wicket by a bowler with chin in hand and eyes agog, ruing the batsman's outrageous stroke of good fortune. See also **Teapot**

Cleaned Up — Of a batsman lavishly bowled

Clothed It — Describing a floppy or poorly executed shot bringing a run or two or costing the fool his wicket. Pronounced as in 'dishcloth'

Clubbed— When a ball is hit jolly hard. See **Biff** for full list of synonyms

Coat of Varnish — Unit of measurement to describe the distance between bat and ball, and ball and wicket. See also **Fag Paper**

Coconut — Batsman's head. As in coconut shy. e.g. *'Ouch! He's worn one right on the coconut there.'*

Coffin — Battered old team kit bag or crate sitting in the village pavilion full of moulding pads, misshapen balls, Victorian batting gloves and broken bats. Like the oldest player in the team, the coffin is much loved but obsolete, and no one has the heart to throw it out

Conker— New ball. Lovely and shiny like the fruit of the Horse Chestnut. See **Cherry**

Good Contest— ... between bat and ball. A well-balanced game, usually used in expressing the eagerness for one

Cooked — Of a fast bowler at the end of a very long spell, often in extreme heat

Corridor of Uncertainty — Poetic, almost perfect phrase understood by every batsman to describe the area outside his off-stump where he has been playing and missing, and beaten all-ends-up

Country Mile, Run Out by a — Laughably long distance by which a batsman has been run out

Cow Corner — Area of the field where **Camels** and **Cart Horses** are left to graze, far from the action

Cow Shot — Shot heaved inelegantly in the hope of a boundary, most often towards Cow Corner

Crackerjack! — Usually prefixed by 'Absolute' and delivered by a commentator in tones of awe to describe a superb ball that has discombobulated the batsman

Crash! Bang! Wallop! — Commentator's doggerel to describe a heavily struck ball or a flurry of shots

Creeper — Nasty surprise of a ball that keeps low often trapping the batsman leg before. One up from a grubber or a shooter that never leaves the ground

Crowd Catch — A six bagged by someone in the stands, triggering gleeful celebrations and the revelation of a massive beer gut as hands shoot aloft

Crown Jewels — *Euph.* See Amidships, Dress Circle, Knackers, Nether Region, Privates

Cue End — See **Chalk End**

Curtly— Long, hard, terrifying stare given by a bowler to a batsman. Named for the great West Indian bowler Curtly Ambrose

Cut Him in Half— Rarely literal. Describing a fast ball that jags back into the batsman at a height between waist and shoulder, triggering panic

D

Dab — Delicate shot, usually behind the wicket, causing surprise and delight amongst onlookers. Not to be confused with the small, bottom-dwelling coastal fish of the North Sea

Daddy Hundred — A term said to be coined or at least popularised by former England captain Graham Gooch describing a substantial century, i.e. one that passes the 150-mark

Dambuster — See **Barnes Wallace**

Dangle a Carrot — What a fast bowler is said to do when he tempts the batsman into a shot with a slightly wide delivery

Dasher — Batsman who doesn't hang about, often an opener, a buccaneer to whom the forward defensive shot is the sign of a timid man not living his life to the full. Criticised for a rash stroke in a tight match, the true dasher will shrug, chortle and tell you, *'Attack is the best form of defence'*

Dead Rubber — Match of no consequence in a series that has been decided by the earlier contests. No one has a clue why it is called a 'rubber'

Death Bowler — Fairly new entry to the cricket lexicon, and exclusive to white-ball cricket, this ghoulish phrase refers to the bowler brought on at the end of an innings, 'at the death', to strangle the flow of runs and kill off the batsmen's hopes of victory

Death Rattle — Wretched sound of leather on the wrong wood heard by a batsman whenever his stumps are rearranged and his life at the crease has been brought to an abrupt end

Decent Shout — Appeal with strong promise, usually when a bowler, bellowing *Howzat?!'* at the umpire, has trapped the batsman leg before

Deck — Another word for pitch, wicket, playing surface, track, strip, or carpet

The Deep — Poetic word for the far outfield just inside the boundary ropes

Demons — A pitch is said to have 'demons' in it for the batsman if it offers prodigious or eccentric bounce to the bowler

Devil's Number — *Aus.* For Australians, eighty-seven is considered to be an unlucky number being thirteen short of a century

Diamond Duck — When a batsman is run out without facing a ball. Also known as a Platinum Duck

Dibbly-dobblies — *Derog.* Harmless deliveries of a commonplace bowler crying out for severe punishment but often inducing caution in a batsman appalled at the prospect of a humiliating dismissal. Usually a part-timer, the purveyor of the dibbly-dobbly will trundle in off a dozen paces and deliver a ball between 60 and 70mph, generally on a length and gun-barrel straight

Dink — Charming term used in the absence of a real word to describe a little shot played into an area untended by a fielder. Shares same word-root as 'dinky'

Dobber — Nothing-ball asking to be malleted to the boundary

Dobbing — Bowler running out a batsman, who is backing up and out of his crease at the non-striker's end, instantly triggering extreme ill-will between the two sides. Perfectly within his rights, the dobber is answerable not to the rules but to his conscience. See also **Mankad**

Doctored — Pitch that has been prepared by the groundsman to exploit the strengths of the home bowling side. Once a cause of moral outrage, doctoring is now considered to be only mildly unsporting - sensible even

Dolly — Pop-up catch to a fielder so easy that Geoff Boycott's mother could pouch it blindfolded while hanging out the washing. Pity the fielder who drops a dolly

Donkey Drop — A ball rarely witnessed beyond the village green or playground, the Donkey Drop soars up in a steep parabola and descends like a space capsule towards the ocean. A laughable spectacle but a curiously difficult ball to play well

Doosra — Off-spinner's take on the googly, the ball surprising the right-handed batsman by turning from leg to off. Meaning the 'second one' or 'other one', the doosra is said to have been invented in the 1960s by the flamboyant Pakistani Prince Aslam Khan who travelled to matches in a Cadillac and fired his revolver to protest umpires' decisions

Dorothy — *Aus.* Rhyming slang for a Six after American Agony Aunt columnist Dorothy Dix

Dot Ball — Delivery from which no run is scored, the expression originating from the match scorer's entry in the record of play. The dot ball is a matter of absolutely no consequence in everyday business but, like the solitary pawn in a tight game of Chess, assumes epic importance in the dying overs of a nail-biting one-day game

Down the Throat — Of a catch hit straight to a fielder. Like a tap-in into an empty football goal, the down-the-throat catch, offering no challenge to the fielder's skills, is a deflating experience rarely followed by jubilant celebrations

Downtown — Massive six smashed back over the head of the bowler heading towards the skyscrapers on the horizon on a jet stream of hyperbole

Drain Bowling — Leaking runs

Draw Stumps — Time-honoured ritual when the umpires collect the bails and pull the three stumps out of the ground at each end to signal the close of play – or when the covers are being raced on during a downpour

Dress Circle — *Euph.* When a ball has struck the batsman smack in the privates. See also **Amidships, Crown Jewels, Knackers, Nether Regions, Privates**. e.g. *'Ouch! Smack in the Dress Circle. That is going to hurt!'*

Drilled it! — Describing a hard shot along the ground that skips over the boundary rope and clatters into the advertising boards before anyone has flinched

Drop Anchor — Policy of a batsman who will be damned if he's going to attempt to score a run. Useful asset in a team of **Dashers,** or in the freefall of a **Calypso Collapso**. Inexcusably dull approach to the art of batting in all other circumstances

Dropsy — Condition suffered by a butter-fingered fielder

Duck — Batsman's score of zero. So called because the numeral is thought to resemble the egg of a duck. Why a duck, and not any other bird, has never been satisfactorily explained. The answer could lie in the first known record of the usage when, in 1866, The Times reported that the Prince of Wales, later Edward VII, returned to the pavilion 'on a duck's egg'

Dustbowl — A pitch baked hard by the sun that has crumbled and turned to dust, giving untold delight to the spin bowler and deep anguish to the batsman. Dustbowls are rarely found in England, but are a common phenomenon in India

E

Economy rate — Nothing to do with monetary policy or GDP, this is simply the average amount of runs conceded per over by a bowler. A good rate depends on the format: Anything under three runs per over for Tests; under six for 50-overs and under eight for T20s

Eddy Extras — Name for the imaginary twelfth batsman accruing wides, no-balls, byes and leg-byes for the team. When 'Eddy' scores big, something is awry in the fielding side. No-balls and wides are the bowlers' shame but a ton of byes points to a poor gloveman. Eddy's highest Test score is 76, chalked up in Pakistan's first innings against India at Bengaluru in 2007

Effort Ball — Delivery born in fury or frustration and delivered with spite. When the fast bowler bends his back in half and vents on the batsman with a **Brute**, often in response to a sluggish pitch or the slight of being hit for a boundary

Effortless — When batting is more art than science, the description of a shot played as though the batsman is on the beach in palm-tree motif swimming trunks with a Daiquiri behind the stumps. Often said of former England captain David Gower's style at the wicket

Enforcer — Fast bowler put on to frighten the **Rabbits** and **Ferrets** and cut down the tail. Bully of the lower orders

Engine — Of a fast bowler happy to put in a shift and bowl long spells as in, *'He's got a good engine on him has Stokesy'*

Engine Room — Middle order of a batting line-up, especially one in the habit of scoring most of the team's runs. Roughly batsmen five to nine

Exchange of Pleasantries — *Euph.* Ugly confrontation at the wicket. A wry euphemism similar to 'handbags' in rugby union describing a hideously violent brawl. The pleasantries exchanged often include expletive references to legitimacy, onanism and the relative beauty of the wife. See **Banter, Chirp, Verbals, Niggle**

Exocet — Extremely fast delivery akin to the French-built anti-ship missile that wreaked a heavy toll on the Royal Navy during the Falklands War of 1982

Eyeball, Giving Him The — Long hard stare by a fast bowler to a batsman who has just fluked him for a boundary or miraculously survived yet another close shave. See **Teapot**

F

Fag Paper — Unit of measurement to describe the distance between bat and ball, and between ball and wicket. See also **Coat of Varnish**

Farm the Strike — Tactic by which the better batsman contrives the play so as to face most of an over, five balls ideally, and protect the useless **Rabbit** or **Ferret** at the other end. The situation usually occurs at the end of a very tight match with the batting side close to a win or hanging on for a draw. To this end, the batsmen decline easy singles. Tense and frustrating to watch

Fast Bowlers' Union — Mythical institution to which all pacemen, regardless of their team loyalty, are said to be members. In the old days, this meant that bowlers did not bowl bumpers at one another. Not so today. With helmets, mutual solicitude about safety in the workplace is a quaint, obsolete convention

Feather, The Merest — Very faint edge to the keeper, often inaudible and only spotted 'upstairs' on **Snicko**

Featherbed — Laughably comfortable wicket for batting. See also **B&B pitch**

Fencing — What a batsman appears to be doing when he swipes and prods haplessly at a delivery outside off-stump

Ferret — Batsman even worse than a **Rabbit**. Expression taken from field sport of hunting with ferrets in which the domesticated polecat is sent in 'after the rabbits'

Filth — Spectacularly poor spell of bowling or a single awful delivery

First Dig — Captain's choice to bat first, usually heard directly after the toss: *'We're gonna have first dig, Naz. The track looks a belter.'*

First Drop — Curious, new-ish, 'cool' expression of uncertain origin, for the batsman coming in at number three. Yes, first in after the fall of an opener, but why 'drop'? Dropdown menu? Philologists are confounded

Fishing — What a batsman is said to be doing when he's casting around outside off-stump in search of the ball

Five-fer — Collective noun. When a batsman has taken five wickets in an innings, the slang just abbreviates the achievement and turns it into a form of word-trophy

Flamingo — Outrageous shot played on one leg cross-swatting a ball from outside off stump over mid-wicket. Mid-shot in a still photo, the batsman bears a dim resemblance to a flamingo, especially with a T20 player wearing pink pyjamas. Shot pioneered by England's Kevin Pietersen

Flash Hard — Quasi-religious instruction by coaches to students of the game around the world. *'If you're gonna flash, lad, flash hard.'* Common sense lies behind the advice: better that a mishit from a swipe outside off-stump flies over the slips towards the ropes than dollies limply to a fielder

Flat Track Bully — Batsman who only scores big runs on a **Featherbed** or **B&B** pitch, and never quite repeats his brilliance on a normal wicket, let alone a difficult one

Flay — What happens when a batsman heeds the advice to **Flash Hard**. Stronger than 'whipped', and on a par with 'lashed', the ball is said to have been flayed to the boundary

Flipper — Leg spinner's variation. A slightly shorter ball with some underspin that keeps lower than the batsman expects, sometimes bowling or rapping him leg before. Invented by Aussie Charlie Grimmett and perfected by the great Shane Warne

Floater — Flighted delivery tossed a little higher and slower with the illusion of it 'floating'

Footler — *Derog.* Harmless, part-time bowler, generally a spinner, bowling **Dibbly-dobblies**

Footwork, Lovely — Sigh of praise for a batsman who uses his feet well to get forward to the pitch of the ball. A high-level skill less coveted since the demise of uncovered pitches and the emergence of the **Featherbed**

Fourth Stump — *Notional.* What a ball would have hit had the 'fourth' stump been real

From Whence it Came — Nonsense expression to describe a ball hammered to the boundary. Illogical because a delivery begins its short life in the hand of the bowler, not the perimeter fence

Frying pans — Wicketkeeper's gloves. Usage rare owing to the poverty of the metaphor

Funky — *Derog.* Possibly *Euph.* Of eccentric bowling or captain's field placement. Foreign Office-speak for 'shit' or 'bewildering'

Furniture — The stumps. To be used only in conjunction with the past tense of 'rearrange'

G

Gardening — Batsman's favourite pastime between overs, ambling down the wicket nonchalantly squashing mostly imaginary tufts and divots in the playing surface. More a mindful, therapeutic exercise than a useful practical one

Gas — Good pace generated by a fast bowler. e.g. '*This lad has got gas! The keeper had to reach for that one!*'

Gate — Space between the batsman's inside edge and the off stump, generally created by a loose shot or by one that has jagged back and **Cut him in Half** or rearranged the **Furniture**

Gimme — Easy catch. See **Dolly**

Giver — Trigger-happy, bowler-friendly umpire, often a former member of the Fast Bowlers' Union. The giver will always look favourably towards the screaming bowler on a tight call for LBW

Glue — Of a player who holds the innings together while his teammates fall apart around him. Loathe to take risks, the 'glue-that-holds-the-innings-together' will often be there at the end, on 42 not out from 112 balls

Golden Duck — Batsman's score when he's out first ball

Gone Big on Him — What a quick ball has done when it rears up from just short of length and gives the batsman a fright

Good Areas — Microgeographic region a bowler has found outside the off-stump. Near perfect line and length. See also **Corridor of Uncertainty**

Good Toss to Lose — When the side put into bat or into the field enjoys the surprising good fortune of the playing surface acting in disobedience to expectations

Good Wheels — Quality a fast bowler is said to possess. Pace. Sometimes shortened to 'wheels'. e.g. *'Woo! That was rapid. The boy's got wheels!'*

Golden Arm — Of an unremarkable weekend bowler in the habit of breaking stubborn partnerships and bagging key wickets to the ceaseless astonishment of his team-mates, and the embarrassment of the pavilion-bound batsman

Googly — Leg spinner's delivery which surprises the right-handed batsman by turning to leg rather than in the stock direction to off. First use of word found in 1904, but its origin is unknown. See also **Bosie**

Got the Wood on Him/Them — *Aus.* Psychological hold exercised by a bowler over a batsman or a whole side over another. Origin uncertain. See also **Bunny**

Grabbers — Those fielding in the slips

Grass it — To drop a catch

Grazing — Untroubled by the core action of the contest, what a fielder in **The Deep** is said to be doing. A gateway activity often leading to dangerous day-dreaming and, *in extremis*, the signing of autographs and the exchange of amusing banter with the crowd

Green Top — Pitch at the start of a match showing a light covering or patches of live grass, causing excitement amongst members of the Fast Bowlers' Union eager to exploit the pronounced movement off the seam that it will bring

Grope — What a batsman is said to be doing when he lazily fondles the air outside off stump, the bat failing to get anywhere near the ball

Grubber — Delivery that shoots along the ground triggering a spasm of alarm in the batsman, often leading to the **Death Rattle** or a rap on his pads. The grubber is not a delivery that can be contrived

Gun — Star player. Origin uncertain. Possibly short for Top Gun, or Big Gun

Gun's Out of the Holster — Tense moment when the umpire's finger emerges from his pocket to condemn the batsman and dispatch him to the pavilion after an appeal for LBW or caught behind

H

Half-tracker — Poor short ball that lands roughly half-way down the 'track' offering the batsman easy runs. See also **Long Hop**

Happy Hooker — Oxymoron describing a batsman who cannot stop himself playing the hook shot but lacks the judgement or technique to execute it with consistent success

Hard Yards — Major effort exerted in a testing period of a game, usually by a fast bowler. A term borrowed from Athletics referring to the final stretch of a race when the body has reached the point of extreme fatigue

Harrow Drive — See **Chinese Cut**

Have a Dart — a) Spontaneous, ill-considered thrust of a batsman towards the ball b) When the fielder shies at the stumps

Heartbeat of the Team — Chirpiest, longest-serving or most valuable player in a side whose mere presence on the pitch or in the pavilion lifts team morale

Heavy Ball — Curiously helpful metaphor describing a very fast delivery, often after it has struck the splice of the bat or the batsmen's gloves when raised to the face in panic defensive mode

Helicopter Shot — A rotational swing of the bat above the head towards the leg side favoured by inept tailenders

High, Wide and Handsome! — Mildly irritating, clumsy but all-too-common exclamation describing a shot lifted over the offside infield to the boundary

Hit & Giggle — Traditionalists' sneering reference to T20 cricket. See also **Pyjama Cricket**

Hit your Straps — *Aus.* To find your best form or enter a hot streak. The origin of the usage is horse-related. When a team of horses in harness is stationary, the leather straps are slack but snap tight when the beasts hit full stride

Hogging — What a batsman is doing when he keeps the strike for himself to the irritation of his batting partner

Hoick — A shot hideous on the eye. **See Agricultural**

Hole Out — To be caught in **The Deep**

Hoodoo — What a bowler is said to hold over a batter he has dismissed many times or who can't lay a bat on him. US alternative for Voodoo. See **Bunny**

Humpty, Give it Some — To strike a ball with tremendous power

Hutch — The pavilion when a batsman is making his way back to it after dismissal

I J K

Inroads — Early progress of a bowling attack through a batting line-up

Inside out — a) State in which a batsman finds himself after contorting his body in reaction to a **Snorter** or **Beauty** b) Batsman's deliberate manoeuvre to convert a leg side ball into an offside shot

Irish swing — *Aus.* Reverse swing. The phenomenon of an old ball being coaxed to swing in the opposite direction to when it was a **Cherry**

...

Jack — a) Slang for a score of nought. Probably abbreviation of jack-shit b) The last batsman as in Nine, Ten, Jack

Jaffa — Brilliant unplayable delivery, usually by a fast bowler that—mostly—does not earn the prize of a wicket it deserves. Jaffa is the Hebrew word for Beautiful

Join Dots — Successive **Dot balls** by a bowler. Tight bowling

Judicious Leave — Curious formal term for a batsman making a sensible decision not to play a shot to a fine delivery travelling close to his off-stump

King Pair — Humiliation of being out for a **Golden Duck** in both innings. A traumatic event—-especially for a top batsman such as India's Virender Sehwag against England in 2011. There have been only 22 King Pairs in almost 150 years of Tests

Knackers — *Euph.* See **Amidships, Crown Jewels, Dress Circle, Nether Regions, Privates**

Knock — Brief, generally useful or attractive innings that does not significantly advance the cause of the batting side but adds a little gaiety to the occasion

Knows Where his Off-stump Is — In reference to the mystical intuitions of a well-organised batsman with exquisite shot selection. The knowing-when-to-leave or to commit to the ball. See **Judicious Leave**

L

Lappa — Indian street word for **Hoick**, an ugly slog over midwicket, neither pull nor sweep, nor fish nor fowl

Lateral Movement — Quasi-scientific description of a ball that is swinging

Lean on/into it — What a batsman does to a ball with no backswing, blocking it with angled bat and letting the pace of the ball do the work

Leggie — Leg-spinner

Length Ball — Delivery placed by the bowler at the appropriate distance from the bat. Expression often used in disdain when a) A batsman has been foolishly dismissed by one or b) In admiration, when he has surprised everyone by punishing it

Lick and Flick — Twin action of fielder cleaning and polishing the ball before tossing it back to the bowler. See also **Spit & Shine**

Lifter — Ball that rises sharply and unexpectedly from a good length

Liquorice Allsorts — *Derog. Hum.* To describe a mish-mash, or irregular assortment, usually of a bowler's spell that has featured some good balls, some bad, some weird. After the old-fashioned British confectionary sold as a mixture in a small paper bag. See also **Bits & Pieces**

Lob Bowling — Familiar sight on the village green, low-quality bowling tossed high in the air, usually pur-veyed by an old cricketer, a very young child or a fat man who struggles to rotate his arm in a natural arc. See **Donkey Drop**

Local Rules — Idiosyncratic, often exasperating laws laid down by a backwoods club with an eccentric ground (e.g. on the slope of a hill, with a tree in the outfield or a farm lane through it)

Lolly or **Lollipop** — a) Soft delivery easily dispatched for runs b) Simple catch

Long Ball, He Hits a — Of a powerful batsman who likes to hit the ball into the stands or over a church

Long Handle, Giving it the — When a batsman launches into the bowling in the search for big runs

Long Hop — Slow short ball, inadvertently delivered, that sits up begging to be smacked hard

Long Levers — Of a batsman with long arms giving him an advantage in striking the ball great distances. It has often been pointed out that England's Kevin Pietersen possesses a pair

Loosener — *Euph.* Awful first ball of a bowler's spell for which he is always forgiven on account of his limbs being stiff and his nerves unsettled

Lusty Blow — *Arch.* Big shot, usually clearing the boundary and often administered by a player of stout girth

M

Maiden — An over unviolated by a batsman's run

Maker's Name — Describing a solid defensive shot, usually on the front foot, played gun-barrel straight and with curt emphasis, allowing the bowler to see clearly the name of the willow's manufacturer

Manhattan — Or **Skyline**. Of the television bar graphic showing the amount of runs scored per over, or per groups of overs, in a one-day game

Mankad — Indian word for **Dobbing**, the controversial act of a bowler running out the non-facing batsman before he has bowled the ball. Named for former Indian all-rounder Vinoo Mankad who caused a terrific hullaballoo when he dobbed a batsman during a Test in Australia in 1947/48

Meat — What a fast bowler hungry for wickets sees when the seventh wicket falls and the rabbits get ready to bat

(In the) Meat — Ball struck cleanly in the centre of the bat

Michelle — Bowler's five-wicket haul, rhyming slang: Five-fer – (Michelle) Pfeiffer, the American film star

Middle — As a verb to describe a shot struck cleanly from the sweet spot of the bat

Military Medium — Borderline *Derog*. Straight-up-and down, moderately paced bowling that troubles no batsman. The sight of the ball being tossed to the master of this non-art comes as a delightful relief to a batsman who has survived the **quicks** or the demon spinner

Minefield — Pitch harbouring multiple dangers for the batsman, usually on days four and five of a Test match after it has deteriorated, and usually found in the spinners' paradise of the sub-continent. See also **Dustbowl**

Missionaries — Lonely distant figures in far-flung outposts of the field far from the busy throb of human affairs

Mongrel, Bit of — Scrapper of a player who will make up for a want of natural talent with an excess of pugnacity manifested in displays of do-or-die fielding, last-bunker batting and a delight in verbal skirmishing

Moon Ball — Delivery tossed towards the heavens. See **Lob Bowling**

Moosed It! — Describing a shot struck with terrific force but without elegance

Mow — To play a big shot without regard to its aesthetic appearance. See also **Hoick, Agricultural**

N

Nelson, On — Score of 111 - either for batsman or a team - considered to be unlucky because the numerals look like stumps without bails. Origin uncertain but thought to relate to Admiral Nelson's loss of various body parts in battle. Test umpire David Shepherd was so superstitious about the Nelson that he used to hop on one leg until the score moved on

Nervous Nineties — Temporary psychological condition of a batsman paralyzed by the realisation he is a couple of shots from a memorable hundred. Stems from understanding that no one will remember him for a score of 93, but a century will bring glory and lasting honour. Pity the eight players dismissed for 99 who never made a Test century

Nether Regions — *Euph.* Genital region. See Also **Amidships, Crown Jewels, Dress Circle, Knackers, Privates**

Net Hero — *Derog.* Disparaging term for a batsman who bestrides and struts the practice nets like a Caesar or

Achilles in a tracksuit, but never scales the same heights of greatness in the heat of battle out in the middle

New Botham — A witch's curse laying an unbearable burden on its victim, causing deep embarrassment to him, and inviting scepticism and ridicule amongst his peers. Cast upon any English player of large frame and belligerent manner who can bat and bowl a bit. Named for peerless and indomitable all-rounder Ian Botham. Most 'New Bothams' are given a couple of caps, then see out their days forgotten in the county backwaters

Nibble — Of bat to a passing ball. A tentative half-shot outside off-stump when the batsman is caught in two minds, or is of timid disposition. The opposite of **Flash Hard**

Niggle — Hostile atmosphere out in the middle often leading to an **Exchange of Pleasantries** between batsman and bowler or a fielder, usually a chirpy wicketkeeper

Nighthawk – A **Nightwatchman** on crack cocaine who comes to the wicket looking to slog 30 runs from 12 balls rather than block 30 balls for one. Term said to be coined by England fast bowler Stuart Broad in the Bazball era of coach Brendon McCullum.

Nightwatchman — Poor sod of limited batting ability from the lower order handed the onerous duty of holding a bowling attack at bay for the last overs of a day's play in order to preserve the superior batsmen for the morrow

Nipbacker — Lazy word for a ball that has jagged into the batsman

Noggin, Wear one on the — Being struck on the helmet or head by a bouncer

No Man's Land — Fielder in a useless position, neither in nor out, often as a result of a captain's 'funky' field placement strategy. See also **Twilight Zone**

No Need — ... to chase that one. A ball that has been struck with such crisp timing or power that the only function of the fielder local to its passage is to go and collect it from beyond the boundary and throw it back to the bowler for a better effort

Notch Up — Accumulate runs in a slow and steady fashion

Nurdle — Homely word describing a shot with no official name by which the batsman manipulates the ball behind the wicket

Nut — Cricket ball or cranium

O

Off for Light — When the umpires oblige the players to leave the field owing to the gathering of dark clouds or the falling of the sun, causing distress and disbelief in the crowd

Office Cricket — Impromptu game at work after the boss has gone home. Use of rulers and balls of paper usually make for an unsatisfying contest, the reality never as much as fun as the idea, and often causing intense irritation to non-participants in the japes. **See also Beach Cricket**

Olympic Rings — Five noughts on a batting scorecard or, rarely, in a batsman's previous five innings at bat

Omelettes —- Or Pizza. Marks left by bowler's run up, emerging slowly in the course of a match

One-Day Shot — Purist or a traditionalist's derision of a vile **Hoick** played in the longer formats of the game

One Skip and Over she Goes — Describing the final leg of a ball driven crisply along the ground and its joyful little dance over the boundary rope

Out of the Screws — Shot struck with awesome power. Expression borrowed from Golf and the age of wooden drivers when a thin metal plate was screwed to the club head. See **Middled**

Out to Graze — Fate of a close fielder after spilling catches, or the leisure of a tired fast bowler, dispatched to **Cow Corner** for some quiet ruminating. Interchangeable with **Out to Pasture**

P Q

Paddle — Gentle shot around the corner in the manner of a novice canoeist

Pastures — Wide-open expanse of the outfield grazed by the fast bowler and the lesser athletic fielder

Peach — Beautiful delivery

Peg back — Of a stump struck by a fast ball or of a scoring rate held in check by tight bowling

Pickpocket — Describing a catch by short-leg, the snaffling fielder an arm's length from the batsman

Pie Chucker — *Derog.* Deeply insulting term describing a bowler of consistently low quality, the caterer of **Buffet Bowling**, highly appetising for the batsman

Pill — Cricket ball, usually in reference to a new or fresh one

Pinch Hitter — Borrowed from Baseball, a hard-hitting batsman brought up from the lower order to accelerate the run-rate

Placement! — Cry of the commentator when a batsman has contrived to pierce the field and direct the ball with exquisite precision

Played down the Piccadilly — … *Should have taken the Bakerloo.* When a batsman wrongly judges the line of the ball with the result of missing it or being dismissed. A reference to the 'lines' of the London Underground network

Playing for his Average — When a batsman prioritises his personal average over the cause of the side, taking few risks and eschewing the team's need of faster runs, or its pursuit of victory. A trait regarded as evidence of a deep moral failing and a solipsistic personality

Plumb — When there can be no doubt that a batsman has been trapped leg before wicket. From 18th century American usage of a 'plumb line' that gives a perfectly straight or exact measurement, a precursor of the spirit level

Poles — *Aus.* The three stumps of a wicket

Polish — Act of rubbing a ball furiously in the groin area of the trousers to achieve more shine, leaving an ugly red and brown smear

Pongo, Take some — Punishment from a sustained and violent batting assault suffered by a bowler or a bowling attack

Popcorn — Easy, more-ish bowling to score off, the idea being the batsman can snack on delivery after delivery, helping himself at will. See **Buffet Bowling**

Popping Crease — Line running across the crease four feet in front of the stumps at both ends of the wicket, over which a bowler must not step, and within which a batsman must keep a part of his body or his bat to avoid being run out or stumped

Pouched — Caught

Powderpuff Delivery — Nothing-ball asking to be spanked by the batsman

Privates – See **Amidships, Crown Jewels, Dress Circle, Knackers, Nether Region**

Pudding — Stodgy or treacly wicket appealing neither to batsman nor bowler

Punishment — What a bowler takes or a batsman administers when the runs are flowing

Purchase, Getting Some — The experience of a spin bowler when his turning balls grip the playing surface, providing encouragement for him and dismay for the batsman

Purist — *Dipl.* Polite term for an old-timer horrified by ongoing changes to the game he loved as a child when wickets were uncovered, men wore pyjamas only at night, and fast bowlers walked or biked the ten miles from their home to the ground for the warm-up. And never complained

Pussy Bowling — Soft bowling. Referring to cats, inviting the batsman's strokes

Put out to Pasture — See **Grazing, Cow Corner**

Put to the Sword — The fate of a single ball, a bowler or an entire team when slain by savage batting

Pyjama Cricket — *Derog. Hum.* T20 cricket. Sniffy reference to the colourful suit of comfortable clothing worn by the players, usually uttered by a **Purist** who prefers his cricket played in flannels, buttoned shirts and hob-nailed boots

Quicks — Fast bowlers or pace attack

Quickie — Hastily-run single

R

Radar — Of a bowler's ability to seek out and hold the correct line and length, the term often used when the system is malfunctioning

Rainbow Throw — Long arcing throw from **The Deep** against the backdrop of the sky

Rapid! — Dramatic o n e - w o r d descriptor of a fast delivery that has startled the commentator as much as the batsman

Real Estate — Untended area of the outfield for the batsman to exploit

Reverse — *Noun.* Short for Reverse swing. Semi-mystical, counter-intuitive phenomenon of an old ball that swings in the opposite direction to which it does when new. A high art perfected and popularized by Pakistan greats Waqar Younis and Wasim Akram

Rib-tickler — *Euph.* Of a savage fast ball that thwacks into a batsman's chest causing eye-watering pain and producing a dark, perfectly circular bruise

Rip — a) Finger effort of a spinner to increase the ball's rotation or b) The commensurate turn in the pitch rewarding the effort

Rip Snorter — Remarkably fast, unplayable short ball that leaps from a length and is worthy of a wicket or threatens decapitation

Ropes — Real and notional, the ropes demarcate the boundary of the playing field, yielding four runs for a ball that crosses them on the ground, a six for one that sails over them without touching the ground

Rough — Battered patch of earth a stride beyond the **Popping Crease** created by a bowler's follow-through, growing in depth and danger for the batsman as the match progresses. Spinners, coming more into a match as the pitch deteriorates, love a bit of rough

S

Schoolboy — *Adj.* of an infantile error committed by a fielder

Scoreboard Pressure — Psychological weight or stress on a batting side when the runs dry up and the required scoring rate increases, often leading to rash strokes and the fall of wickets

Scratching About — Like a hen in a barren farmyard, to describe a batsman out of form or out of his comfort zone, flailing to land bat on ball or hit it beyond the square

Screws on, Put the — To go hard at the batters with stringent bowling and aggressive fielding, stemming the runs, upping the pressure and, in modern parlance, getting 'in the face' of the opposition. Derives from Thumbscrew, an instrument of Medieval torture popular in Scotland

Scythed — Slashed or cut hard off the back foot usually into the off-side in the uncouth manner of a peasant at harvest time. See **Agricultural**

Senior Players — Most experienced or the best players in a team, sometimes forming a ruling clique and referred to as 'the Seniors' by the less notable players with the use of aerial inverted commas

Shank — To mishit or mistime a ball, often with the toe end of the bat or off the splice. Always ugly, often a lucky escape

Shell — To drop a catch, like a peeled pea popping from its pod

Shirtfront — Flat, easy wicket to bat on, like a well-pressed, starched dress shirt with no imperfections to encourage the bowler

Short Arm Jab — To punch a shot with minimal back lift. As in Boxing, the shot is executed with a lightning-fast dart

Shoulder Arms — *Mil.* Defensive movement by the batsman, lifting his arms above his head, adjudging that a ball carries too much risk to play. Different from a 'leave' where he simply ignores a ball carrying no threat. There are few more tragi-comic sights in cricket than a batsman shouldering arms only to have his **Furniture** rearranged

Silly — Of any fielding position close to the bat, or of a spectator's fancy dress costume

Sitter — Easy catching chance. As in 'sitting duck'

Skid On — Of a ball that bounces a bit lower than expected to the surprise of the batsman

Skier — Poorly executed shot that flies high into the air, presenting the fielder underneath it with a tense few seconds while it makes its descent through the atmosphere. See **Snow On**

Sledge — Ancient Australian tradition of mocking and taunting a batsman in order to unsettle him and effect his 'mental disintegration' by reference to his form, looks and wife (© Steve Waugh). Origin unverifiable but strongest claim is story of Aussie players taunting player about his wife and singing the Percy Sledge song 'When a Man Loves a Woman.' See **Banter, Chirp, Exchange of Pleasantries, Niggle, Verbals**

Slider — Another word for a **Flipper** in which a leg-spinner's flatter delivery shoots on at a lower trajectory with the aim of winning an LBW shout

Slot, In the — Ball served up on the perfect line and length for the batsman to strike straight back over or past the bowler

Smear — Ugly shot or one hit with tremendous force

Smoked — Of a ball dispatched to boundary with such speed it might as well be on fire, like a spacecraft re-entering the atmosphere, See **Biff for all synonyms**

Snaffle — Catch with quick reactions

Snicko — Short for Snickometer, a frame-by-frame televisual system to determine whether the ball has snicked the edge of the bat and the batsman can be adjudged caught behind if he has, or possibly leg before if he hasn't. Term remains embedded in cricket jargon in spite of the adoption of Ultra Edge, a more advanced and accurate system

Sniff the Leather — Poetic phrase describing the terror experienced by a batsman when a fast ball rockets past his face

Snow On It — Erroneous meteorological analogy to describe a ball that has been struck very high into the atmosphere. Erroneous because a) Cricket is a summer sport, played mostly in hot climates b) Snow clouds are usually low

Soft Hands — Of a shot played with delicacy, usually dabbed behind the wicket through the close fielders

Speed Merchant — Purveyor of very quick bowling

Spear In — When a fast ball is angled into the boots. See **Yorker**

Spit & Shine — See **Lick and Flick**

Square — Central area of the playing field with the playing surface at its heart and where the grass has been cultivated and manicured to a higher quality than the outfield. Example: '*Poor chap, can't hit it off the square today.*'

Start the Car, Time to — *Hum.* To signal the imminent end of an innings or match. A more colourful way of saying 'It's all over' for the side facing defeat

Steady the Ship — What a batsman or partnership does after a stormy period of play has resulted in the loss of multiple hands on the **Deck**

Steepler — Fanciful description of a ball that has been hit into the air high as a church steeple. See **Skier, Snow On It**

Steepling — Of a delivery that rises at an unexpectedly sharp almost perpendicular angle in the manner of a church steeple from the Late English Gothic period

Sticky Dog — Rare phenomenon in modern professional cricket with pitches being covered, but common at village and club level where the playing surface remains exposed to the elements. A delight for bowlers, a wet wicket is commensurately difficult for the batsman and harder still if the sun has emerged to render it a treacly mess

Stick of Rhubarb — In respect of bowling so poor that Sir Geoffrey Boycott's mother could make whoopee with it using no more than a stalk of this edible hardy perennial. Boycott grew up in the 'Rhubarb Triangle', a nine-square mile area near Wakefield famous for its production of early forced rhubarb

Stodger — Batsman who scores slowly on account of incompetence or risk aversion

Stonewaller — A blocker. A batsman who comes to the crease with no intention other than to deny the bowler a wicket, offering no strokes but the defensive one. A frustrating adversary for the bowler

Strangle — What bowlers do to batsmen when they bowl a tight line and length and severely limit the flow of runs. The mounting pressure is heightened by aggressive fielding and judicious field placement

Street — Easy wicket for batters. Or, Road, Highway

Streetwise — Describing a team or a player who, like a Dickensian pickpocket or a New York mugger, shows an alertness to or, an instinctive awareness for, an opportunity

Strip — Pitch or wicket on which the game is being played out. See also **Deck, Track**

Strong Arm — Quality of an outfielder with a long, powerful throw that makes a batsman think twice about risking an extra run, knowing the ball will be delivered hard, flat and accurately to the stumps

Sultan of Swing — Particularly impressive exponent of the art of coaxing the ball to move into or away from the batsman as a result of its aerodynamic properties rendered by keeping one side rough and the other highly polished. A term that entered the cricket lexicon after the 1978 release of Dire Straits' classic rock track 'Sultans of Swing'

Surgical — Batsman's dissection of the field with a shot so fingertip-neat and precise it might just as well have been carried out by the Surgeon-General with a scalpel

Swat — Contemptuous, inelegant shot, usually for a boundary, when a batsman chooses function over form and the commentator cries, *'They all count!'* and the purist cringes

Sweet Spot — Spongy centre of the bat found by the batsman as the ball races to the ropes. See **Out of the Screws, Middled**

Swingers' Paradise — Cricket ground where the ball moves around a great deal in the air to the delight of fast and medium pacers, and the despair of opening batsmen

Swinging like a Rusty Gate — Of a batsman hopelessly out of touch swiping his bat in vain at a succession of balls

T

Tail — The bottom end of a batting line-up as in 'The tail is wagging.'

Tail-up — Of a fast bowler in optimistic mood because a) He has bagged a couple of wickets and senses there are more for the taking, b) The wicket is bowler-friendly and promises a day of fun, or c) He was born like that

Tap, Bit of — *Euph.* What a bowler suffers when he has been carted all around the ground

Teapot — Posture struck by a disgruntled bowler: hand on hip in disbelief or disgust as yet another ball just misses the wicket or outside edge, yet another catch has been dropped or yet another Chinese Cut has sped away for four. The Double Teapot— both hands on hips— augurs an **Exchange of Pleasantries**

Terror Track — Distressingly dangerous wicket for the batsman on account of a) Low-quality groundsmanship or b) Sinister plot to load the match in favour of the home side's battery of quicks

Textbook — Of a classically executed shot as satisfying to witness as to play, bringing gasps of delight from the traditionalist and the junior batting coach

Thinking Captain — Of a skipper demonstrably reflective in his decision-making, identifiable by a knitted brow, slow stroking of the chin and his love of a three-man huddle during play

Think Out — What a bowler is said to do to a batsman by the intelligence of his delivery selection. Usually, that's three short ones followed by a yorker. Also, of a bearded captain who moves a fielder into a position where a catch is taken soon afterwards

Throat Ball — Horrible rising delivery that threatens to tear out the windpipe of the batsman, often resulting in an ungainly tangle of his limbs and the loss of his balance

Through the Gate — Of a delivery that finds its way between the batsman's inside edge and his pads leading, but not always, to the disturbing of his stumps

Ticker — Heroic and stoic. The quality a batsman displays in a daunting or dangerous match situation or on a **Terror Track**. Sometimes said of a player who brings courage to his game but little else

Tickle — Batsman's playful caress of a ball off his pads, around the corner towards Fine Leg for a gentle run or two and occasionally for four

Tidy Over — Term of praise in the shorter forms of the game where run economy is prized, but mildly derogatory in Test cricket, indicating that the bowler may have kept the ball in the right spot but has troubled the batsman not at all

Timber/s — The (wooden) stumps especially when they have been felled by a swingeing delivery. Also of the (willow) bat, as in *'That's a heavy stick of timber he is swinging!'*

Toe-smasher —Fast yorker into the feet of the batsman

Tonk — Hit hard in a playful, carefree fashion

Tonto — Batsman playing a less important role to the putative Lone Ranger dominating the play or hogging the strike at the other end

Trademark Shot — Signature attacking shot with which a batsman scores a great many of his runs, often a push off his legs through midwicket or a guided cut behind square. The usage is diplomatic when the shot is the only one of note in the batsman's repertoire

Trap — a) When a bowler pins the batsman's leg before and there can be no doubt about his fate or b) Into which an unwary batsman falls after a cunning ruse by a **Thinking Captain** who has moved a fielder a few yards

Treatment, Give the — Batsman's brutal execution of a ball to the boundary. See also **Give it Some Tap**

Triggered — a) When the umpire, quick on the draw, pulls his 'trigger' finger like a gunfighter, terminating the batsman's life at the crease or b) A bowler's very bad mood occasioned by gross ill-fortune or ill-treatment

Trimmer — A delivery that shaves the stumps

Trundler — *Derog.* Slow-witted bowler of limited gifts, usually a **Bits-and-Pieces** player. Traipses to the wicket like a lazy hick to a barn dance and delivers a folksy medium-paced ball. Once in a harvest moon he will dupe the over-eager batsman into a rash shot

Tuck up — Surprising a batsman with a ball that rears off a length or jags back, hurrying him into an emergency defensive shot

Turner — Wicket offering the spin bowler plenty of encouragement. See **Dustbowl, Bunsen**

Turn your arm over? — Usually posed as an interrogative by a captain to a **Trundler** in order to make him feel an important part of the proceedings

Tweaker — Inferior finger spinner. See also **Twiddler**

Twelfth Man — Player not good enough to make the starting XI, or his skills deemed unsuitable for the conditions. Duties in a Test are tedious and thankless: long days on the iPhone, jogs to the middle with fresh gloves or tape, fielding in short bursts for a fast bowler 'receiving treatment', always having to look eager and delighted to be a part of the camp— and, in the shorter forms, suffering the indignity of wearing a high-viz vest

Twiddler — *Derog.* Spin bowler of no account

Two-eyed Stance — Unorthodox, ugly batting posture in which the batsman stands more square-on to the bowler, provoking grumbles from the armchair purist

U

Umbrella Field — Beautiful sight, especially at Lord's, often seen on the first morning of a Test, the grass green, the cherry fresh, and a cordon of six or seven close fielders aligned in an arc between wicketkeeper and the square as the opening bowler starts his run-up

Under the Pump — Team, or a player, subjected to enormous pressure. Origin uncertain. Also, Under the Gun, Under the Kosh

Up Periscope — Confused metaphor for a batsman ducking under a fast bouncer with his bat in a vertical position. (When a submarine dives, the periscope is retracted not extended.) Origin possibly vulgar, referring to a man's state of arousal in the bath or hot tub

Uppish — A mild admonishment. Of a ball struck a few yards above the ground, carrying the risk of being caught if repeated again

Upstairs, Go — When a player, team or on-field umpire makes use of the Decision Review System (DRS) and goes to the third umpire 'upstairs' in his little technology cabin to appeal against, or check, an on-field decision. The batsman or fielding captain will signal the request by making a 'T' letter with their hands; the umpire draws a crude television set in the air

V

Venom — Of a single fast and nasty ball delivered, or - of a fast bowler's spell

Verbals — Abusive exchange between batsman and bowler and/or the close fielders. The introduction of stump microphones has obliged the most potty-mouthed players to clean up their verbals, at least within public earshot. See Also **Niggle, Exchange of Pleasantries, Banter**

Village — *Derog.* Amateurish, low quality. Used to describe a single crass act, or the general ineptitude of a team's performance featuring a flurry of dropped catches, comical fielding errors and rank bowling

Vultures — The gaggle of close fielders around a lowly, helpless batsman or, when the death of an innings is imminent, and the spinner is making it spit and twist

Wahoo, Bit of a — Inelegant, hard swipe at the ball, making no contact, often with head in the air, as with a clown performing a cricket skit at the circus. See also **Village, Agricultural, Hoick**

Wag — When the tail end of the batting order gets in on the runs, usually with a swagger and often to the embarrassment of the specialists back in the pavilion

Walking Wicket — Extremely poor batsman whose journey from pavilion to middle will take longer than his innings

Wang — Lazy word for a lazy bowling action or the manner of a delivery. Bowl without thought or style

Wagon Wheel — Like a pie chart, a televisual graphic broken down into slices to show the areas of the pitch where the batsman has scored his runs. Rarely of great interest to the viewer, it helps give the television coverage a scientific, in-depth feel while saying little more than, 'A few on the leg, a few on the off'

War Paint — The thick band of sunblock striped across the bridge of the nose much favoured by fast bowlers in an effort to look menacing

Wear a Ball — *Euph.* To be struck by a fast ball, suffer unspeakable pain and shock, and have to feign indifference

Weigh Anchor — Of a batsman advancing cautiously or stuck in the doldrums who suddenly launches into the bowlers and starts playing some shots

Welly, Give it Some — Farmyard term to describe uncouth batting. See also **Agricultural**

Wheels Coming Off — Of a batting side, often after a fast start, first spluttering and slowing, then falling apart and crashing

Willow Wand — Childish, irritating term for a bat, often used by a batsman suffering delusions about the magic he can conjure with it

Windmill — Expansive shot played off the front foot in which the batsman's whirling arms will propel the bat in a near-360 degree rotation. Ugly on the eye, but highly effective if contact is made

Without Troubling the Scorers — Pooterish term describing a batsman making the return journey to the pavilion having scored no runs

Wobble Seam — A seamer's mystery delivery that unsettles and surprises the batsman by the unpredict-ability of its movement off the pitch. The effect, always accidental, is achieved by the bowler's irregular grip of the ball

Work Horse — Unflattering term for a seamer who makes up for a want of skill by a commitment to run himself into the ground for the team. Often poorly rewarded for his tireless efforts, rarely with more than two wickets to show for a long day in harness under the ceaseless crack of the batsman's whip

Worm — Crude television graph showing an upwardly diagonal line illustrating a batting team's run-scoring rate against overs bowled, often lumped on top of a separate coloured squiggling worm from the earlier innings. The scale being too great to reveal telling data, the effect is one of an idle child's drawing, undermining the broadcaster's conceit of providing cutting-edge analysis

Wristy — Of an especially supple batsman or deftly played stroke

Wrong 'un — *Aus.* **Googly, Bosie**

X Y Z

X-factor — Mythical quality of an otherwise mediocre player who magics small triumphs out of nowhere— a blinding catch, a clever run-out, a gem of an innings or a couple of crucial wickets at a key moment in the game

Yard — Unit of measurement, or what the physicists call a 'scalar', to describe a ball that has travelled a bit quicker than the average. As in, *'That one's hurried the batsman there. It was a yard or two quicker.'*

Yips — Bizarre, unfathomable neurological disorder afflicting bowlers who lose the ability, once natural and easy to them, to find their line and length. A phenomenon found across hand-eye coordination sports, cases can be so severe as to terminate good careers

Yorker — A fast ball fired into the **Blockhole** at the batsman's boots, upsetting his footwork and often finding a way under the bat to hit the stumps.

See **Toesmasher**

...

Zip — A ball delivered with some extra pace

Zone, In the — Zenlike flow of a player performing as though on automatic pilot or in a magical trance

Acknowledgements

Glancing at the cover and flicking through the book's contents will reveal a score of exceptional, distinctive illustrations. I'm not going to jinx her by calling her the 'New Botham' of Illustration, but Mudd Bexley is a major young talent. Undoubtedly, you will see a great deal more of her work in the years to come. Her illustrations here perfectly capture the book's humorous tone – and, though no Badger, she 'got it' from the start. She is also highly efficient and professional: give her a suggestion or a task at sunrise, and you will always be examining an assortment of options by sunset - and often by high noon. Check out more of her work on Instagram @izustrations

Major thanks as well to the design team of Rebecca and Andrew Brown from Design for Writers, who came highly recommended by word of mouth and excelled themselves on every score. They have been doing brilliant work for authors and other creators for fifteen years. It being 2024 and living at different ends of England, we haven't met, and we probably never will, but they have been a joy to work with. I hope we work together again. Model professionals, highly knowledgeable and generous with broader publishing guidance, they have been imaginative, helpful and efficient in equal measure in producing this book.

About the Author

Niall Edworthy is one of the UK's leading ghostwriters. He started his career as a cricket reporter for the Independent on Sunday before joining the international wire agency AFP and later Reuters, reporting on news and sport.

He began writing books in 1997. His first was a history of the England football team, the second a history of Lord's cricket ground, and his first collaborative project, a book with the Only Fools and Horses actor David Jason.

He has since written over forty titles, the majority of them ghosted for well-known names: actors, musicians, sportsmen & television personalities, but also several notable servicemen and 'ordinary' people with extraordinary stories to tell.

His first novel, *Otto Eckhart's Ordeal*, was shortlisted for the Wilbur Smith Best Published Novel Award 2021. He has recently finished his second novel. He lives in West Sussex, UK, and embarrasses himself every summer on cricket grounds across the county.

Contact: niall@nialledworthy.com

NIALLEDWORTHY.COM

Printed in Great Britain
by Amazon